2ND GRADE DOUBLE DIGITS VERTICAL ADDITION DRILL WORKBOOK

CHILDREN'S MATH BOOKS

Speedy Publishing LLC
40 E. Main St. #1156
Newark, DE 19711
www.speedypublishing.com

Practice your addition skills with this workbook and this will help you love math even more.

Have Fun Learning Kid!

SET 1

Addition of 2 Digits, 2 Addends

SET 1

EXERCISE NO. 1

Name: ....

Date: .... Score: ....

1.) $\begin{array}{r} 34 \\ +\ 54 \\ \hline \end{array}$

2.) $\begin{array}{r} 15 \\ +\ 94 \\ \hline \end{array}$

3.) $\begin{array}{r} 89 \\ +\ 48 \\ \hline \end{array}$

4.) $\begin{array}{r} 15 \\ +\ 46 \\ \hline \end{array}$

5.) $\begin{array}{r} 74 \\ +\ 54 \\ \hline \end{array}$

6.) $\begin{array}{r} 76 \\ +\ 81 \\ \hline \end{array}$

7.) $\begin{array}{r} 65 \\ +\ 77 \\ \hline \end{array}$

8.) $\begin{array}{r} 92 \\ +\ 69 \\ \hline \end{array}$

SET 1

EXERCISE NO. 2

Name: ....

Date: .... Score: ....

1.) 25 + 50 = ____

2.) 10 + 15 = ____

3.) 32 + 24 = ____

4.) 74 + 89 = ____

5.) 23 + 23 = ____

6.) 32 + 93 = ____

7.) 66 + 96 = ____

8.) 15 + 72 = ____

SET 1

EXERCISE NO. 3

1.) $\begin{array}{r} 10 \\ +\ 28 \\ \hline \end{array}$

2.) $\begin{array}{r} 33 \\ +\ 31 \\ \hline \end{array}$

3.) $\begin{array}{r} 80 \\ +\ 97 \\ \hline \end{array}$

4.) $\begin{array}{r} 19 \\ +\ 96 \\ \hline \end{array}$

5.) $\begin{array}{r} 82 \\ +\ 43 \\ \hline \end{array}$

6.) $\begin{array}{r} 74 \\ +\ 59 \\ \hline \end{array}$

7.) $\begin{array}{r} 16 \\ +\ 90 \\ \hline \end{array}$

8.) $\begin{array}{r} 37 \\ +\ 65 \\ \hline \end{array}$

SET 1

EXERCISE NO. 4

Name: ....

Date: .... Score: ....

1.) $\begin{array}{r} 17 \\ +\ 22 \\ \hline \end{array}$

2.) $\begin{array}{r} 87 \\ +\ 57 \\ \hline \end{array}$

3.) $\begin{array}{r} 18 \\ +\ 74 \\ \hline \end{array}$

4.) $\begin{array}{r} 18 \\ +\ 88 \\ \hline \end{array}$

5.) $\begin{array}{r} 48 \\ +\ 39 \\ \hline \end{array}$

6.) $\begin{array}{r} 79 \\ +\ 62 \\ \hline \end{array}$

7.) $\begin{array}{r} 76 \\ +\ 14 \\ \hline \end{array}$

8.) $\begin{array}{r} 97 \\ +\ 98 \\ \hline \end{array}$

SET 1

EXERCISE NO. 5

1.) 85 + 69 = ___

2.) 47 + 30 = ___

3.) 35 + 79 = ___

4.) 88 + 15 = ___

5.) 99 + 27 = ___

6.) 67 + 74 = ___

7.) 10 + 55 = ___

8.) 49 + 40 = ___

SET 1

EXERCISE NO. 6

Name: ....

Date: .... Score: ....

1.) 38 + 74 = ____

2.) 65 + 10 = ____

3.) 16 + 75 = ____

4.) 35 + 31 = ____

5.) 95 + 29 = ____

6.) 53 + 19 = ____

7.) 87 + 35 = ____

8.) 73 + 95 = ____

EXERCISE NO. 7

1.) $14 + 69$

2.) $20 + 83$

3.) $83 + 45$

4.) $64 + 88$

5.) $77 + 31$

6.) $99 + 60$

7.) $17 + 91$

8.) $73 + 11$

SET 1

EXERCISE NO. 8

Name: ....

Date: .... Score: ....

1.) 31 + 32

2.) 20 + 54

3.) 58 + 29

4.) 70 + 42

5.) 44 + 19

6.) 27 + 86

7.) 14 + 46

8.) 74 + 70

SET 1

EXERCISE NO. 9

1.) 56 + 21 = ____

2.) 78 + 29 = ____

3.) 76 + 11 = ____

4.) 76 + 13 = ____

5.) 76 + 93 = ____

6.) 61 + 94 = ____

7.) 42 + 35 = ____

8.) 45 + 55 = ____

SET 1

EXERCISE NO. 10

Name: ....

Date: .... Score: ....

1.) $\begin{array}{r} 56 \\ +\ 79 \\ \hline \end{array}$

2.) $\begin{array}{r} 99 \\ +\ 39 \\ \hline \end{array}$

3.) $\begin{array}{r} 48 \\ +\ 61 \\ \hline \end{array}$

4.) $\begin{array}{r} 17 \\ +\ 41 \\ \hline \end{array}$

5.) $\begin{array}{r} 71 \\ +\ 88 \\ \hline \end{array}$

6.) $\begin{array}{r} 75 \\ +\ 70 \\ \hline \end{array}$

7.) $\begin{array}{r} 16 \\ +\ 67 \\ \hline \end{array}$

8.) $\begin{array}{r} 85 \\ +\ 70 \\ \hline \end{array}$

GOOD
JOB!

SET 2

Addition of 2 Digits, 3 Addends

SET 2

EXERCISE NO. 1

1.)
```
   47
   47
 + 94
 ----
```

2.)
```
   70
   29
 + 78
 ----
```

3.)
```
   45
   38
 + 95
 ----
```

4.)
```
   89
   67
 + 27
 ----
```

5.)
```
   81
   33
 + 60
 ----
```

6.)
```
   28
   78
 + 15
 ----
```

7.)
```
   72
   98
 + 69
 ----
```

8.)
```
   81
   78
 + 25
 ----
```

SET 2

EXERCISE NO. 2

Name: ....

Date: .... Score: ....

1.) 63 + 56 + 25 =

$$\begin{array}{r} 63 \\ 56 \\ +\ 25 \\ \hline \end{array}$$

2.)

$$\begin{array}{r} 61 \\ 46 \\ +\ 73 \\ \hline \end{array}$$

3.)

$$\begin{array}{r} 64 \\ 16 \\ +\ 96 \\ \hline \end{array}$$

4.)

$$\begin{array}{r} 62 \\ 78 \\ +\ 18 \\ \hline \end{array}$$

5.)

$$\begin{array}{r} 45 \\ 39 \\ +\ 28 \\ \hline \end{array}$$

6.)

$$\begin{array}{r} 74 \\ 93 \\ +\ 69 \\ \hline \end{array}$$

7.)

$$\begin{array}{r} 74 \\ 47 \\ +\ 11 \\ \hline \end{array}$$

8.)

$$\begin{array}{r} 90 \\ 57 \\ +\ 27 \\ \hline \end{array}$$

SET 2

EXERCISE NO. 3

1.)
$$\begin{array}{r} 65 \\ 37 \\ +\ 97 \\ \hline \end{array}$$

2.)
$$\begin{array}{r} 29 \\ 47 \\ +\ 10 \\ \hline \end{array}$$

3.)
$$\begin{array}{r} 78 \\ 62 \\ +\ 54 \\ \hline \end{array}$$

4.)
$$\begin{array}{r} 35 \\ 36 \\ +\ 72 \\ \hline \end{array}$$

5.)
$$\begin{array}{r} 93 \\ 57 \\ +\ 28 \\ \hline \end{array}$$

6.)
$$\begin{array}{r} 86 \\ 68 \\ +\ 58 \\ \hline \end{array}$$

7.)
$$\begin{array}{r} 22 \\ 40 \\ +\ 88 \\ \hline \end{array}$$

8.)
$$\begin{array}{r} 94 \\ 41 \\ +\ 48 \\ \hline \end{array}$$

SET 2

EXERCISE NO. 4

Name: ....

Date: .... Score: ....

1.) $\begin{array}{r} 41 \\ 99 \\ +\ 31 \\ \hline \end{array}$

2.) $\begin{array}{r} 63 \\ 68 \\ +\ 87 \\ \hline \end{array}$

3.) $\begin{array}{r} 45 \\ 29 \\ +\ 67 \\ \hline \end{array}$

4.) $\begin{array}{r} 37 \\ 99 \\ +\ 21 \\ \hline \end{array}$

5.) $\begin{array}{r} 60 \\ 94 \\ +\ 51 \\ \hline \end{array}$

6.) $\begin{array}{r} 72 \\ 60 \\ +\ 94 \\ \hline \end{array}$

7.) $\begin{array}{r} 64 \\ 40 \\ +\ 59 \\ \hline \end{array}$

8.) $\begin{array}{r} 33 \\ 69 \\ +\ 27 \\ \hline \end{array}$

SET 2

EXERCISE NO. 5

1.)
$$\begin{array}{r} 18 \\ 56 \\ +\ 78 \\ \hline \end{array}$$

2.)
$$\begin{array}{r} 33 \\ 36 \\ +\ 57 \\ \hline \end{array}$$

3.)
$$\begin{array}{r} 27 \\ 38 \\ +\ 49 \\ \hline \end{array}$$

4.)
$$\begin{array}{r} 88 \\ 69 \\ +\ 65 \\ \hline \end{array}$$

5.)
$$\begin{array}{r} 96 \\ 87 \\ +\ 95 \\ \hline \end{array}$$

6.)
$$\begin{array}{r} 68 \\ 38 \\ +\ 96 \\ \hline \end{array}$$

7.)
$$\begin{array}{r} 45 \\ 16 \\ +\ 15 \\ \hline \end{array}$$

8.)
$$\begin{array}{r} 18 \\ 68 \\ +\ 63 \\ \hline \end{array}$$

SET 2

EXERCISE NO. 6

Name: ....

Date: .... Score: ....

1.) 22 + 91 + 81 = ____

2.) 47 + 84 + 18 = ____

3.) 22 + 98 + 87 = ____

4.) 47 + 33 + 78 = ____

5.) 80 + 75 + 53 = ____

6.) 23 + 13 + 54 = ____

7.) 21 + 32 + 35 = ____

8.) 83 + 10 + 50 = ____

SET 2

EXERCISE NO. 7

1.)
$$\begin{array}{r} 99 \\ 16 \\ +\ 47 \\ \hline \end{array}$$

2.)
$$\begin{array}{r} 98 \\ 49 \\ +\ 39 \\ \hline \end{array}$$

3.)
$$\begin{array}{r} 36 \\ 36 \\ +\ 14 \\ \hline \end{array}$$

4.)
$$\begin{array}{r} 82 \\ 35 \\ +\ 81 \\ \hline \end{array}$$

5.)
$$\begin{array}{r} 59 \\ 73 \\ +\ 35 \\ \hline \end{array}$$

6.)
$$\begin{array}{r} 36 \\ 44 \\ +\ 25 \\ \hline \end{array}$$

7.)
$$\begin{array}{r} 75 \\ 22 \\ +\ 68 \\ \hline \end{array}$$

8.)
$$\begin{array}{r} 54 \\ 70 \\ +\ 32 \\ \hline \end{array}$$

SET 2

EXERCISE NO. 8

Name: ....

Date: .... Score: ....

1.) $\begin{array}{r} 14 \\ 30 \\ +\ 46 \\ \hline \end{array}$	2.) $\begin{array}{r} 46 \\ 93 \\ +\ 25 \\ \hline \end{array}$	3.) $\begin{array}{r} 37 \\ 27 \\ +\ 54 \\ \hline \end{array}$	4.) $\begin{array}{r} 82 \\ 64 \\ +\ 92 \\ \hline \end{array}$
5.) $\begin{array}{r} 62 \\ 98 \\ +\ 75 \\ \hline \end{array}$	6.) $\begin{array}{r} 90 \\ 37 \\ +\ 14 \\ \hline \end{array}$	7.) $\begin{array}{r} 10 \\ 43 \\ +\ 64 \\ \hline \end{array}$	8.) $\begin{array}{r} 98 \\ 26 \\ +\ 49 \\ \hline \end{array}$

SET 2

EXERCISE NO. 9

1.) 24 + 12 + 21 =

$$\begin{array}{r} 24 \\ 12 \\ +\ 21 \\ \hline \end{array}$$

2.)

$$\begin{array}{r} 41 \\ 99 \\ +\ 50 \\ \hline \end{array}$$

3.)

$$\begin{array}{r} 23 \\ 91 \\ +\ 95 \\ \hline \end{array}$$

4.)

$$\begin{array}{r} 50 \\ 49 \\ +\ 40 \\ \hline \end{array}$$

5.)

$$\begin{array}{r} 54 \\ 98 \\ +\ 87 \\ \hline \end{array}$$

6.)

$$\begin{array}{r} 75 \\ 29 \\ +\ 41 \\ \hline \end{array}$$

7.)

$$\begin{array}{r} 58 \\ 50 \\ +\ 78 \\ \hline \end{array}$$

8.)

$$\begin{array}{r} 77 \\ 23 \\ +\ 42 \\ \hline \end{array}$$

SET 2

EXERCISE NO. 10

Name: ....

Date: .... Score: ....

1.) 87 + 64 + 97 = ____

2.) 66 + 66 + 41 = ____

3.) 62 + 67 + 54 = ____

4.) 20 + 87 + 83 = ____

5.) 39 + 46 + 69 = ____

6.) 41 + 64 + 78 = ____

7.) 39 + 25 + 22 = ____

8.) 94 + 42 + 37 = ____

SET 2

EXERCISE NO. 11

1.)
$$\begin{array}{r} 37 \\ 53 \\ +\ 26 \\ \hline \end{array}$$

2.)
$$\begin{array}{r} 74 \\ 58 \\ +\ 75 \\ \hline \end{array}$$

3.)
$$\begin{array}{r} 87 \\ 37 \\ +\ 39 \\ \hline \end{array}$$

4.)
$$\begin{array}{r} 42 \\ 62 \\ +\ 39 \\ \hline \end{array}$$

5.)
$$\begin{array}{r} 22 \\ 22 \\ +\ 64 \\ \hline \end{array}$$

6.)
$$\begin{array}{r} 24 \\ 15 \\ +\ 42 \\ \hline \end{array}$$

7.)
$$\begin{array}{r} 26 \\ 32 \\ +\ 66 \\ \hline \end{array}$$

8.)
$$\begin{array}{r} 51 \\ 92 \\ +\ 31 \\ \hline \end{array}$$

SET 2

EXERCISE NO. 12

Name: ....

Date: .... Score: ....

1.)
$$\begin{array}{r} 64 \\ 29 \\ +\ 59 \\ \hline \end{array}$$

2.)
$$\begin{array}{r} 22 \\ 83 \\ +\ 80 \\ \hline \end{array}$$

3.)
$$\begin{array}{r} 55 \\ 39 \\ +\ 63 \\ \hline \end{array}$$

4.)
$$\begin{array}{r} 60 \\ 22 \\ +\ 48 \\ \hline \end{array}$$

5.)
$$\begin{array}{r} 51 \\ 67 \\ +\ 33 \\ \hline \end{array}$$

6.)
$$\begin{array}{r} 43 \\ 21 \\ +\ 35 \\ \hline \end{array}$$

7.)
$$\begin{array}{r} 54 \\ 17 \\ +\ 67 \\ \hline \end{array}$$

8.)
$$\begin{array}{r} 87 \\ 86 \\ +\ 41 \\ \hline \end{array}$$

SET 2

EXERCISE NO. 13

1.)
$$\begin{array}{r} 88 \\ 92 \\ +\ 19 \\ \hline \end{array}$$

2.)
$$\begin{array}{r} 68 \\ 68 \\ +\ 82 \\ \hline \end{array}$$

3.)
$$\begin{array}{r} 12 \\ 43 \\ +\ 51 \\ \hline \end{array}$$

4.)
$$\begin{array}{r} 70 \\ 97 \\ +\ 95 \\ \hline \end{array}$$

5.)
$$\begin{array}{r} 18 \\ 90 \\ +\ 59 \\ \hline \end{array}$$

6.)
$$\begin{array}{r} 83 \\ 33 \\ +\ 27 \\ \hline \end{array}$$

7.)
$$\begin{array}{r} 15 \\ 70 \\ +\ 70 \\ \hline \end{array}$$

8.)
$$\begin{array}{r} 94 \\ 28 \\ +\ 74 \\ \hline \end{array}$$

SET 2

EXERCISE NO. 14

Name: ....

Date: .... Score: ....

1.) 83 + 30 + 53 = ____

2.) 95 + 84 + 40 = ____

3.) 30 + 85 + 41 = ____

4.) 35 + 25 + 90 = ____

5.) 75 + 31 + 32 = ____

6.) 15 + 65 + 21 = ____

7.) 16 + 44 + 90 = ____

8.) 46 + 56 + 97 = ____

SET 2

EXERCISE NO. 15

1.) $\begin{array}{r} 31 \\ 38 \\ +\ 26 \\ \hline \end{array}$

2.) $\begin{array}{r} 42 \\ 36 \\ +\ 59 \\ \hline \end{array}$

3.) $\begin{array}{r} 68 \\ 75 \\ +\ 68 \\ \hline \end{array}$

4.) $\begin{array}{r} 72 \\ 33 \\ +\ 23 \\ \hline \end{array}$

5.) $\begin{array}{r} 82 \\ 57 \\ +\ 70 \\ \hline \end{array}$

6.) $\begin{array}{r} 56 \\ 76 \\ +\ 20 \\ \hline \end{array}$

7.) $\begin{array}{r} 58 \\ 34 \\ +\ 95 \\ \hline \end{array}$

8.) $\begin{array}{r} 21 \\ 74 \\ +\ 61 \\ \hline \end{array}$

Excellent!

SET 3

Addition of 2 Digits, 4 Addends

SET 3

EXERCISE NO. 1

Name: ....

Date: .... Score: ....

1.)
```
   22
   96
   88
+  27
-----
```

2.)
```
   90
   88
   54
+  73
-----
```

3.)
```
   57
   68
   16
+  24
-----
```

4.)
```
   85
   97
   36
+  50
-----
```

5.)
```
   88
   20
   98
+  74
-----
```

6.)
```
   58
   78
   74
+  28
-----
```

7.)
```
   13
   55
   51
+  58
-----
```

8.)
```
   81
   53
   86
+  73
-----
```

EXERCISE NO. 2

1.)
93
17
16
+ 31

2.)
55
65
59
+ 10

3.)
79
75
83
+ 27

4.)
65
60
48
+ 58

5.)
45
53
76
+ 33

6.)
24
11
99
+ 37

7.)
48
95
89
+ 82

8.)
51
27
82
+ 85

SET 3

EXERCISE NO. 3

Name: ....

Date: .... Score: ....

1.)	2.)	3.)	4.)
34	34	18	53
71	14	58	73
58	43	41	78
+ 84	+ 26	+ 65	+ 46

5.)	6.)	7.)	8.)
91	80	38	72
89	12	79	32
20	75	85	98
+ 30	+ 26	+ 14	+ 15

SET 3

EXERCISE NO. 4

1.) 31 + 87 + 26 + 76 =

2.) 46 + 69 + 14 + 71 =

3.) 35 + 71 + 35 + 51 =

4.) 84 + 65 + 75 + 45 =

5.) 94 + 19 + 67 + 25 =

6.) 32 + 17 + 51 + 16 =

7.) 25 + 10 + 40 + 25 =

8.) 52 + 57 + 62 + 11 =

SET 3

EXERCISE NO. 5

Name: ....

Date: .... Score: ....

1.) 45
65
15
+ 61

2.) 45
70
99
+ 83

3.) 43
33
81
+ 59

4.) 15
99
99
+ 83

5.) 71
12
27
+ 61

6.) 38
11
35
+ 57

7.) 92
14
97
+ 75

8.) 17
41
61
+ 27

SET 3

EXERCISE NO. 6

1.) 77 + 43 + 71 + 57 = ____

2.) 56 + 91 + 58 + 99 = ____

3.) 30 + 89 + 78 + 66 = ____

4.) 67 + 89 + 33 + 77 = ____

5.) 55 + 55 + 82 + 92 = ____

6.) 98 + 43 + 66 + 90 = ____

7.) 18 + 28 + 73 + 33 = ____

8.) 34 + 40 + 99 + 57 = ____

SET 3

EXERCISE NO. 7

Name: ....

Date: .... Score: ....

1.)	2.)	3.)	4.)
97	84	64	42
54	98	55	72
53	82	86	46
+ 42	+ 85	+ 97	+ 19

5.)	6.)	7.)	8.)
72	22	81	96
85	64	44	65
38	15	16	81
+ 23	+ 67	+ 65	+ 29

SET 3

EXERCISE NO. 8

1.) 31, 35, 74, + 15

2.) 61, 40, 66, + 38

3.) 53, 97, 78, + 31

4.) 24, 54, 38, + 55

5.) 95, 83, 24, + 31

6.) 39, 57, 65, + 52

7.) 90, 33, 55, + 89

8.) 15, 22, 22, + 90

SET 3

EXERCISE NO. 9

Name: ....

Date: .... Score: ....

1.)
```
  80
  47
  71
+ 69
----
```

2.)
```
  47
  72
  72
+ 97
----
```

3.)
```
  42
  49
  68
+ 88
----
```

4.)
```
  90
  44
  22
+ 47
----
```

5.)
```
  71
  35
  84
+ 32
----
```

6.)
```
  62
  50
  31
+ 85
----
```

7.)
```
  79
  11
  95
+ 12
----
```

8.)
```
  73
  41
  12
+ 76
----
```

EXERCISE NO. 10

1.) 74
94
79
\+ 29

2.) 42
21
91
\+ 77

3.) 70
73
14
\+ 71

4.) 48
40
80
\+ 87

5.) 71
11
44
\+ 10

6.) 37
59
72
\+ 41

7.) 52
61
55
\+ 14

8.) 15
78
95
\+ 82

SET 3

EXERCISE NO. 11

Name: ....

Date: .... Score: ....

1.) 85 + 32 + 55 + 82 = ____

2.) 17 + 91 + 11 + 15 = ____

3.) 92 + 40 + 14 + 52 = ____

4.) 16 + 27 + 67 + 56 = ____

5.) 33 + 30 + 46 + 30 = ____

6.) 39 + 43 + 47 + 56 = ____

7.) 76 + 84 + 16 + 77 = ____

8.) 16 + 51 + 70 + 71 = ____

SET 3

EXERCISE NO. 12

1.)	2.)	3.)	4.)
20	71	54	74
74	86	97	92
83	61	73	70
+ 91	+ 20	+ 97	+ 30

5.)	6.)	7.)	8.)
66	36	44	33
77	56	51	74
48	70	91	91
+ 28	+ 22	+ 93	+ 75

SET 3

EXERCISE NO. 13

Name: ....

Date: .... Score: ....

1.)	2.)	3.)	4.)
36	41	52	67
11	11	46	66
11	78	93	91
+ 38	+ 16	+ 88	+ 77

5.)	6.)	7.)	8.)
85	36	95	37
66	58	73	15
45	25	98	29
+ 82	+ 48	+ 53	+ 98

SET 3

EXERCISE NO. 14

1.)	2.)	3.)	4.)
37	41	90	20
48	80	20	93
27	43	85	11
+ 99	+ 61	+ 51	+ 10

5.)	6.)	7.)	8.)
74	52	49	82
83	59	89	21
93	75	63	66
+ 80	+ 78	+ 77	+ 84

SET 3

EXERCISE NO. 15

Name: ....

Date: .... Score: ....

1.) 47 + 39 + 76 + 62 = ____

2.) 81 + 45 + 37 + 13 = ____

3.) 37 + 63 + 65 + 87 = ____

4.) 97 + 61 + 61 + 68 = ____

5.) 91 + 93 + 51 + 58 = ____

6.) 19 + 18 + 25 + 74 = ____

7.) 34 + 35 + 97 + 84 = ____

8.) 89 + 97 + 84 + 71 = ____

Great Job Kid!

AWESOME!

Addition is Fun Right? Keep on learning!

ANSWERS

SET 1

Addition of 2 Digits, 2 Addends

SET 1 — EXERCISE NO. 1

Name: ....

Date: .... Score: ....

1.] $\begin{array}{r} 34 \\ +\,54 \\ \hline 88 \end{array}$	2.] $\begin{array}{r} 15 \\ +\,94 \\ \hline 109 \end{array}$	3.] $\begin{array}{r} 89 \\ +\,48 \\ \hline 137 \end{array}$	4.] $\begin{array}{r} 15 \\ +\,46 \\ \hline 61 \end{array}$
5.] $\begin{array}{r} 74 \\ +\,54 \\ \hline 128 \end{array}$	6.] $\begin{array}{r} 76 \\ +\,81 \\ \hline 157 \end{array}$	7.] $\begin{array}{r} 65 \\ +\,77 \\ \hline 142 \end{array}$	8.] $\begin{array}{r} 92 \\ +\,69 \\ \hline 161 \end{array}$

SET 1 — EXERCISE NO. 2

Name: ....

Date: .... Score: ....

1.] $\begin{array}{r} 25 \\ +\,50 \\ \hline 75 \end{array}$	2.] $\begin{array}{r} 10 \\ +\,15 \\ \hline 25 \end{array}$	3.] $\begin{array}{r} 32 \\ +\,24 \\ \hline 56 \end{array}$	4.] $\begin{array}{r} 74 \\ +\,89 \\ \hline 163 \end{array}$
5.] $\begin{array}{r} 23 \\ +\,23 \\ \hline 46 \end{array}$	6.] $\begin{array}{r} 32 \\ +\,93 \\ \hline 125 \end{array}$	7.] $\begin{array}{r} 66 \\ +\,96 \\ \hline 162 \end{array}$	8.] $\begin{array}{r} 15 \\ +\,72 \\ \hline 87 \end{array}$

SET 1 — EXERCISE NO. 3

Name: ....

Date: .... Score: ....

1.] $\begin{array}{r} 10 \\ +\,28 \\ \hline 38 \end{array}$	2.] $\begin{array}{r} 33 \\ +\,31 \\ \hline 64 \end{array}$	3.] $\begin{array}{r} 80 \\ +\,97 \\ \hline 177 \end{array}$	4.] $\begin{array}{r} 19 \\ +\,96 \\ \hline 115 \end{array}$
5.] $\begin{array}{r} 82 \\ +\,43 \\ \hline 125 \end{array}$	6.] $\begin{array}{r} 74 \\ +\,59 \\ \hline 133 \end{array}$	7.] $\begin{array}{r} 16 \\ +\,90 \\ \hline 106 \end{array}$	8.] $\begin{array}{r} 37 \\ +\,65 \\ \hline 102 \end{array}$

SET 1 — EXERCISE NO. 4

Name: ....

Date: .... Score: ....

1.)	2.)	3.)	4.)
17 + 22 = 39	87 + 57 = 144	18 + 74 = 92	18 + 88 = 106

5.)	6.)	7.)	8.)
48 + 39 = 87	79 + 62 = 141	76 + 14 = 90	97 + 98 = 195

SET 1 — EXERCISE NO. 5

Name: ....

Date: .... Score: ....

1.)	2.)	3.)	4.)
85 + 69 = 154	47 + 30 = 77	35 + 79 = 114	88 + 15 = 103

5.)	6.)	7.)	8.)
99 + 27 = 126	67 + 74 = 141	10 + 55 = 65	49 + 40 = 89

SET 1 — EXERCISE NO. 6

Name: ....

Date: .... Score: ....

1.)	2.)	3.)	4.)
38 + 74 = 112	65 + 10 = 75	16 + 75 = 91	35 + 31 = 66

5.)	6.)	7.)	8.)
95 + 29 = 124	53 + 19 = 72	87 + 35 = 122	73 + 95 = 168

SET 1 — EXERCISE NO. 7

Name: ....

Date: .... Score: ....

1.)	2.)	3.)	4.)
14 + 69 = 83	20 + 83 = 103	83 + 45 = 128	64 + 88 = 152

5.)	6.)	7.)	8.)
77 + 31 = 108	99 + 60 = 159	17 + 91 = 108	73 + 11 = 84

SET 1 — EXERCISE NO. 8

Name: ....

Date: .... Score: ....

1.) 31 + 32 = 63

2.) 20 + 54 = 74

3.) 58 + 29 = 87

4.) 70 + 42 = 112

5.) 44 + 19 = 63

6.) 27 + 86 = 113

7.) 14 + 46 = 60

8.) 74 + 70 = 144

SET 1 — EXERCISE NO. 9

Name: ....

Date: .... Score: ....

1.) 56 + 21 = 77

2.) 78 + 29 = 107

3.) 76 + 11 = 87

4.) 76 + 13 = 89

5.) 76 + 93 = 169

6.) 61 + 94 = 155

7.) 42 + 35 = 77

8.) 45 + 55 = 100

SET 1 — EXERCISE NO. 10

Name: ....

Date: .... Score: ....

1.) 56 + 79 = 135

2.) 99 + 39 = 138

3.) 48 + 61 = 109

4.) 17 + 41 = 58

5.) 71 + 88 = 159

6.) 75 + 70 = 145

7.) 16 + 67 = 83

8.) 85 + 70 = 155

SET 2

Addition of 2 Digits, 3 Addends

SET 2 — EXERCISE NO. 1

Name: ....
Date: .... Score: ....

1.)	2.)	3.)	4.)
47	70	45	89
47	29	38	67
+ 94	+ 78	+ 95	+ 27
188	177	178	183

5.)	6.)	7.)	8.)
81	28	72	81
33	78	98	78
+ 60	+ 15	+ 69	+ 25
174	121	239	184

SET 2 — EXERCISE NO. 2

Name: ....
Date: .... Score: ....

1.)	2.)	3.)	4.)
63	61	64	62
56	46	16	78
+ 25	+ 73	+ 96	+ 18
144	180	176	158

5.)	6.)	7.)	8.)
45	74	74	90
39	93	47	57
+ 28	+ 69	+ 11	+ 27
112	236	132	174

SET 2 — EXERCISE NO. 3

Name: ....
Date: .... Score: ....

1.)	2.)	3.)	4.)
65	29	78	35
37	47	62	36
+ 97	+ 10	+ 54	+ 72
199	86	194	143

5.)	6.)	7.)	8.)
93	86	22	94
57	68	40	41
+ 28	+ 58	+ 88	+ 48
178	212	150	183

SET 2 — EXERCISE NO. 3

Name: ....
Date: .... Score: ....

1.)	2.)	3.)	4.)
65	29	78	35
37	47	62	36
+ 97	+ 10	+ 54	+ 72
199	86	194	143

5.)	6.)	7.)	8.)
93	86	22	94
57	68	40	41
+ 28	+ 58	+ 88	+ 48
178	212	150	183

SET 2 — EXERCISE NO. 4

Name: ....

Date: .... Score: ....

1.) 41 + 99 + 31 = 171	2.) 63 + 68 + 87 = 218	3.) 45 + 29 + 67 = 141	4.) 37 + 99 + 21 = 157
5.) 60 + 94 + 51 = 205	6.) 72 + 60 + 94 = 226	7.) 64 + 40 + 59 = 163	8.) 33 + 69 + 27 = 129

SET 2 — EXERCISE NO. 5

Name: ....

Date: .... Score: ....

1.) 18 + 56 + 78 = 152	2.) 33 + 36 + 57 = 126	3.) 27 + 38 + 49 = 114	4.) 88 + 69 + 65 = 222
5.) 96 + 87 + 95 = 278	6.) 68 + 38 + 96 = 202	7.) 45 + 16 + 15 = 76	8.) 18 + 68 + 63 = 149

SET 2 — EXERCISE NO. 6

Name: ....

Date: .... Score: ....

1.) 22 + 91 + 81 = 194	2.) 47 + 84 + 18 = 149	3.) 22 + 98 + 87 = 207	4.) 47 + 33 + 78 = 158
5.) 80 + 75 + 53 = 208	6.) 23 + 13 + 54 = 90	7.) 21 + 32 + 35 = 88	8.) 83 + 10 + 50 = 143

SET 2 — EXERCISE NO. 7

Name: ....

Date: .... Score: ....

1.) 99 + 16 + 47 = 162	2.) 98 + 49 + 39 = 186	3.) 36 + 36 + 14 = 86	4.) 82 + 35 + 81 = 198
5.) 59 + 73 + 35 = 167	6.) 36 + 44 + 25 = 105	7.) 75 + 22 + 68 = 165	8.) 54 + 70 + 32 = 156

SET 2 — EXERCISE NO. 8

Name: ....
Date: .... Score: ....

1.]	2.]	3.]	4.]
14	46	37	82
30	93	27	64
+ 46	+ 25	+ 54	+ 92
90	164	118	238

5.]	6.]	7.]	8.]
62	90	10	98
98	37	43	26
+ 75	+ 14	+ 64	+ 49
235	141	117	173

SET 2 — EXERCISE NO. 9

Name: ....
Date: .... Score: ....

1.]	2.]	3.]	4.]
24	41	23	50
12	99	91	49
+ 21	+ 50	+ 95	+ 40
57	190	209	139

5.]	6.]	7.]	8.]
54	75	58	77
98	29	50	23
+ 87	+ 41	+ 78	+ 42
239	145	186	142

SET 2 — EXERCISE NO. 10

Name: ....
Date: .... Score: ....

1.]	2.]	3.]	4.]
87	66	62	20
64	66	67	87
+ 97	+ 41	+ 54	+ 83
248	173	183	190

5.]	6.]	7.]	8.]
39	41	39	94
46	64	25	42
+ 69	+ 78	+ 22	+ 37
154	183	86	173

SET 2 — EXERCISE NO. 11

Name: ....
Date: .... Score: ....

1.]	2.]	3.]	4.]
37	74	87	42
53	58	37	62
+ 26	+ 75	+ 39	+ 39
116	207	163	143

5.]	6.]	7.]	8.]
22	24	26	51
22	15	32	92
+ 64	+ 42	+ 66	+ 31
108	81	124	174

SET 2 — EXERCISE NO. 12

Name: ....

Date: .... Score: ....

1.)	2.)	3.)	4.)
64	22	55	60
29	83	39	22
+ 59	+ 80	+ 63	+ 48
152	185	157	130

5.)	6.)	7.)	8.)
51	43	54	87
67	21	17	86
+ 33	+ 35	+ 67	+ 41
151	99	138	214

SET 2 — EXERCISE NO. 13

Name: ....

Date: .... Score: ....

1.)	2.)	3.)	4.)
88	68	12	70
92	68	43	97
+ 19	+ 82	+ 51	+ 95
199	218	106	262

5.)	6.)	7.)	8.)
18	83	15	94
90	33	70	28
+ 59	+ 27	+ 70	+ 74
167	143	155	196

SET 2 — EXERCISE NO. 14

Name: ....

Date: .... Score: ....

1.)	2.)	3.)	4.)
83	95	30	35
30	84	85	25
+ 53	+ 40	+ 41	+ 90
166	219	156	150

5.)	6.)	7.)	8.)
75	15	16	46
31	65	44	56
+ 32	+ 21	+ 90	+ 97
138	101	150	199

SET 3

Addition of 2 Digits, 4 Addends

SET 3 — EXERCISE NO. 1

Name: ....
Date: .... Score: ....

1.)	2.)	3.)	4.)
22	90	57	85
96	88	68	97
88	54	16	36
+ 27	+ 73	+ 24	+ 50
233	305	165	268

5.)	6.)	7.)	8.)
88	58	13	81
20	78	55	53
98	74	51	86
+ 74	+ 28	+ 58	+ 73
280	238	177	293

SET 3 — EXERCISE NO. 2

Name: ....
Date: .... Score: ....

1.)	2.)	3.)	4.)
93	55	79	65
17	65	75	60
16	59	83	48
+ 31	+ 10	+ 27	+ 58
157	189	264	231

5.)	6.)	7.)	8.)
45	24	48	51
53	11	95	27
76	99	89	82
+ 33	+ 37	+ 82	+ 85
207	171	314	245

SET 3 — EXERCISE NO. 3

Name: ....
Date: .... Score: ....

1.)	2.)	3.)	4.)
34	34	18	53
71	14	58	73
58	43	41	78
+ 84	+ 26	+ 65	+ 46
247	117	182	250

5.)	6.)	7.)	8.)
91	80	38	72
89	12	79	32
20	75	85	98
+ 30	+ 26	+ 14	+ 15
230	193	216	217

SET 3 — EXERCISE NO. 4

Name: ....
Date: .... Score: ....

1.)	2.)	3.)	4.)
31	46	35	84
87	69	71	65
26	14	35	75
+ 76	+ 71	+ 51	+ 45
220	200	192	269

5.)	6.)	7.)	8.)
94	32	25	52
19	17	10	57
67	51	40	62
+ 25	+ 16	+ 25	+ 11
205	116	100	182

SET 3 — EXERCISE NO. 5

Name: ....

Date: .... Score: ....

1.)	2.)	3.)	4.)
45	45	43	15
65	70	33	99
15	99	81	99
+ 61	+ 83	+ 59	+ 83
186	297	216	296

5.)	6.)	7.)	8.)
71	38	92	17
12	11	14	41
27	35	97	61
+ 61	+ 57	+ 75	+ 27
171	141	278	146

SET 3 — EXERCISE NO. 6

Name: ....

Date: .... Score: ....

1.)	2.)	3.)	4.)
77	56	30	67
43	91	89	89
71	58	78	33
+ 57	+ 99	+ 66	+ 77
248	304	263	266

5.)	6.)	7.)	8.)
55	98	18	34
55	43	28	40
82	66	73	99
+ 92	+ 90	+ 33	+ 57
284	297	152	230

SET 3 — EXERCISE NO. 7

Name: ....

Date: .... Score: ....

1.)	2.)	3.)	4.)
97	84	64	42
54	98	55	72
53	82	86	46
+ 42	+ 85	+ 97	+ 19
246	349	302	179

5.)	6.)	7.)	8.)
72	22	81	96
85	64	44	65
38	15	16	81
+ 23	+ 67	+ 65	+ 29
218	168	206	271

SET 3 — EXERCISE NO. 8

Name: ....

Date: .... Score: ....

1.)	2.)	3.)	4.)
31	61	53	24
35	40	97	54
74	66	78	38
+ 15	+ 38	+ 31	+ 55
155	205	259	171

5.)	6.)	7.)	8.)
95	39	90	15
83	57	33	22
24	65	55	22
+ 31	+ 52	+ 89	+ 90
233	213	267	149

SET 3 — EXERCISE NO. 9

Name: ....
Date: .... Score: ....

1.)	2.)	3.)	4.)
80	47	42	90
47	72	49	44
71	72	68	22
+ 69	+ 97	+ 88	+ 47
267	288	247	203

5.)	6.)	7.)	8.)
71	62	79	73
35	50	11	41
84	31	95	12
+ 32	+ 85	+ 12	+ 76
222	228	197	202

SET 3 — EXERCISE NO. 10

Name: ....
Date: .... Score: ....

1.)	2.)	3.)	4.)
74	42	70	48
94	21	73	40
79	91	14	80
+ 29	+ 77	+ 71	+ 87
276	231	228	255

5.)	6.)	7.)	8.)
71	37	52	15
11	59	61	78
44	72	55	95
+ 10	+ 41	+ 14	+ 82
136	209	182	270

SET 3 — EXERCISE NO. 11

Name: ....
Date: .... Score: ....

1.)	2.)	3.)	4.)
85	17	92	16
32	91	40	27
55	11	14	67
+ 82	+ 15	+ 52	+ 56
254	134	198	166

5.)	6.)	7.)	8.)
33	39	76	16
30	43	84	51
46	47	16	70
+ 30	+ 56	+ 77	+ 71
139	185	253	208

SET 3 — EXERCISE NO. 12

Name: ....
Date: .... Score: ....

1.)	2.)	3.)	4.)
20	71	54	74
74	86	97	92
83	61	73	70
+ 91	+ 20	+ 97	+ 30
268	238	321	266

5.)	6.)	7.)	8.)
66	36	44	33
77	56	51	74
48	70	91	91
+ 28	+ 22	+ 93	+ 75
219	184	279	273

SET 3 — EXERCISE NO. 13

Name: ....

Date: .... Score: ....

1.)	2.)	3.)	4.)
36	41	52	67
11	11	46	66
11	78	93	91
+ 38	+ 16	+ 88	+ 77
96	146	279	301

5.)	6.)	7.)	8.)
85	36	95	37
66	58	73	15
45	25	98	29
+ 82	+ 48	+ 53	+ 98
278	167	319	179

SET 3 — EXERCISE NO. 14

Name: ....

Date: .... Score: ....

1.)	2.)	3.)	4.)
37	41	90	20
48	80	20	93
27	43	85	11
+ 99	+ 61	+ 51	+ 10
211	225	246	134

5.)	6.)	7.)	8.)
74	52	49	82
83	59	89	21
93	75	63	66
+ 80	+ 78	+ 77	+ 84
330	264	278	253

SET 3 — EXERCISE NO. 15

Name: ....

Date: .... Score: ....

1.)	2.)	3.)	4.)
47	81	37	97
39	45	63	61
76	37	65	61
+ 62	+ 13	+ 87	+ 68
224	176	252	287

5.)	6.)	7.)	8.)
91	19	34	89
93	18	35	97
51	25	97	84
+ 58	+ 74	+ 84	+ 71
293	136	250	341

www.ingramcontent.com/pod-product-compliance
Lightning Source LLC
LaVergne TN
LVHW060826170826
845678LV00010B/1913

* 9 7 9 8 8 6 9 4 4 4 4 5 5 *